THE UNICORN AT THE MANGER

THE UNICORN AT THE MANGER

Yearlong Stories of the Holy Night

&

Roger L. Robbennolt

UNITED CHURCH PRESS

Cleveland, Ohio

United Church Press, Cleveland, Ohio 44115

© 1996 by Roger L. Robbennolt

Biblical quotations are from the New Revised Standard Version of the Bible, © 1989 by

the Division of Christian Education of the National Council of the Churches of Christ

in the U.S.A., and are used by permission

Published 1996. All rights reserved

Printed in the United States of America on acid-free paper

01 00 99 98 97 96   5 4 3 2 1

LIBRARY OF CONGRESS CATALOGING-IN-PUBLICATION DATA

Robbennolt, Roger.
    The unicorn at the manger : yearlong stories of the Holy Night /
Roger L. Robbennolt.
        p.   cm.
    ISBN 0-8298-1146-x (alk. paper)
        1. Jesus Christ—Nativity—Fiction.   2. Christian fiction, American.
3. Christmas stories, American.   I. Title.
    PS3568.02224U55   1996
    813'.54—dc20   96-9658
                                                                CIP

for

Lucy Linker, who started it all

The Community of Shantivanam / Forest of Peace Press,
who gave me a reason to write again

The congregation of First Congregational Church (UCC),
Walla Walla, Washington,
who encouraged, endured, and loved these tales
out of my heart's depths

Contents

A Prologue of Sorts

"ROG, I THINK WE NEED a new crèche before next Christmas Eve. Every church should have a manger scene. We've never had a really fine one."

The afternoon sun of late July flooded our study, obliterating thoughts of Christmas. My wife, Pat, and I had arrived seven months earlier to be co-pastors of the church. We were scrambling to move the congregation in some fresh directions. We were into overarching concepts. At the moment I was confronted by a beloved church member with a deep-running need to be a gift-giver.

"That's not a top priority at the moment, Lucy. It would be lovely, but there's no money in the church budget. I'm also concerned that simplicity be the order of the day when considering such an item."

She persisted. "I'm doing some ceramic art. I'd love to create a crèche. I've taken the liberty of bringing an example of how it might be fired."

She placed upon my desk a small unicorn.

It looked at me quizzically. I returned its gaze. I started to comment on its exquisite firing, but the room was empty. A woman of infinite wisdom, Lucy knew when to leave a man alone with his unicorn.

I was taken aback by his opening salvo. "I'm a bit afraid of you," he began. "I sense you to be a very angry man. My all-knowingness gives me all the details of your troubled past, but they are unimportant. If you listen deeply during our time together, you may learn something about gentleness."

I bristled defensively. Then I felt myself starting to cry. I sensed that the unicorn and I were about to begin a strange journey together.

A few weeks later the crèche arrived. It was a single large unit. All the requisite figures were there, glowing in their simplicity. I turned the stable around to get another perspective. I nearly dropped it!

There, staring at me through a rude opening in the crude abode, was a grim-faced cow. It was obvious she didn't like me—or much else in all creation. The feeling was mutual. The vibrations between us were dreadful!

I muttered my thanks to Lucy for her most excellent offering, while being totally discomfited by the cow. I slipped the stable and its attendant parts into a box, which I shelved in a dark corner under the office sink. I can confess it now: I rather hoped it might be forgotten.

I returned to my desk to commune with the unicorn—and to write a note to Lucy begging forgiveness for my brusqueness and thanking her for her splendid gift. The unicorn smiled.

Christmas Eve morning arrived. The phone rang. It was Lucy, reminding me that the manger scene's inauguration was to happen that very evening.

I headed for the illicit hiding place. It was still there. The crèche would occupy a place of honor on a low chancel table, soon to be surrounded by admiring children.

As I robed for the service, I realized that I wasn't fully prepared for the sacred festivities. I shared my fears with the unicorn. He always seemed to understand.

I moved from our desk, turned off the study lights, and started through the door. Then I looked back. A full December moon shone on the little unicorn. In the shifting shadows, he appeared to have lowered his golden horn, and straining his neck forward, seemed to be trying to rise to his golden hooves and follow me.

No one should ever desert a unicorn on Christmas Eve. Removing my car keys from my pocket, I picked up the little beast and held him for a moment in the palm of my great rough hand. The moon-light glistened on a tear running down his cheek.

I gently placed him in my pocket and hurried to the back of the sanctuary. I stepped into the processional, drawn forward by the marching motifs of "O Come, O Come Emmanuel." The unicorn was nestled contentedly against my thigh.

A few minutes into the service the children came tumbling down the aisle for their special story. They gathered around Lucy's candlelit crèche.

To my amazement, the following tale poured from my pocket and my heart.

The Unicorn at the Manger

YOU WERE PROBABLY UNAWARE of the fact that the stable behind the inn at Bethlehem was completely controlled by the cow.

She was the bossiest of beasts. Order and reason were the hallmarks of her being. Her left horn curled a bit longer than her right. Imagination was the preserve only of children and poets, neither of which were allowed near her domain.

The donkey had to go to a far pasture if she was to bray. The resident ram had to wipe his hooves carefully before entering. The ox was requested to brush dust from his hide on bushes by the door. All the stable's inhabitants were completely cowed by the cow.

Imagine her consternation when great crowds began to flood the Bethlehem streets. Chaos was in the air.

All the animals felt impending uncertainty. The donkey brayed in the cow's ear, and the cow responded with a sharp kick to her leg. The poor donkey limped sadly to a dark corner.

The impossible appeared in the person of the innkeeper, who bustled into the cow's special space and, without even consulting her, ushered in an exhausted man and an apprehensive young woman far along in her pregnancy. He assured them they could spend the night sleeping on straw. Then he disappeared.

The couple settled near the ox's manger. The woman moaned. The cow, having birthed six calves, knew that another being was about to enter the ordered confines of her particular corner of the universe.

There was a deep moan, a tiny cry, and a joy-choked shout from the man: "A boy! A boy! A holy boy!"

Then it happened. Even the rational cow moved uncomfortably close to an appreciation of the miraculous. A burst of light illumined the stable.

She saw a great star beaming through the ventilation hole in the roof and shining onto the couple, who wrapped the child in swaddling cloths as they laid him in the manger.

Her concern deepened as she heard the murmur of voices. She saw shepherds peering through openings in the wall. Even the cow felt their awe.

She sprang into action. She nudged them into kneeling positions around the manger. Behind the scene she arranged the donkey, the ram, and the ox—with herself carefully in the center.

As serenity returned she thought, "Perfect order, perfect balance! We'll all look lovely on Christmas cards."

Then she heard it: the clip-clop, clip-clop of tiny hooves on the cobblestones. Looking down the street, she saw a unicorn running toward the stable in the starlight.

The fatigue of the day had frayed the cow's nerves. In spite of herself she shouted, "Away with you, unicorn! There's no room at the manger for a mythological beast!"

Her shout awakened the baby. Though everyone sensed his holiness, he screamed at the top of his small lungs. Nothing the young mother did quieted him.

The cow was beside herself. Not only was the crying disturbing the animal occupants and shepherd guests, but the unicorn had dared to ignore her command.

He steadfastly trotted toward the stable door, pushed his way past the gawking shepherds, and completely disarranged the cow's splendid scenic symmetry.

As the unicorn gazed in wonder at the squalling child, he saw with his mystic eyes the sacred encased within the decidedly human.

At that moment, the intensity of starlight struck his golden horn. The stable ceiling exploded with reflected diamonds of light. With an infinitesimal movement of the unicorn's head, the diamonds danced.

The dancing diamonds caught the attention of the crying child. He quieted abruptly. His eyes followed the cascades of light playing across the cedar beams.

Doves in the rafters, awakened by the transformation of their night into day, began to coo with joy. Their sound was echoed by the babe in the straw.

For the first time in her life the cow was dumbfounded. A mythological beast could bring peace to the child. She caught the unicorn's eye and, with a sweep of her imperious head, gave him permission to join the shepherds and their sheep in the tableau of worship.

The unicorn knelt at the manger. He did not even mind when the cow nudged him slightly to the left.

The Interlude of the Lion

THE CHURCH COUNCIL SAT around the oak table that August evening. Someone mentioned Christmas.

Lucy, the church clerk, smiled. "I have a present for Rog."

She handed me a box wrapped in red with an appropriate sprig of plastic holly.

She continued, "It's an addition to the crèche."

I opened the package with some hesitation. A ferocious lion nervously lay in its unaccustomed surroundings of white tissue paper. Its face was deeply lined.

He was dutifully passed around the table and admired. Someone commented, "He looks a bit psychotic."

The moderator looked down the table at me and said, "I see the wheels turning in Rog's mind. I think Christmas Eve is coming into focus."

I took the lion into our study and introduced him to the unicorn, who now occupied a permanent place of honor on the corner of my desk. I thought the horned beast involuntarily flinched. The lion looked a bit too interested in the fat little animal. I put the lion in the box with the rest of the Christmas objects.

A week later I sat in my desk chair for a few moments before an early appointment. I turned to greet the unicorn and my heart sank. Its golden horn had been snapped off. A vandal had taken a red pen and drawn blood on the injured stump.

I wept for the unicorn—and for the rage in the human heart that sullies so much of creation with such desecrations.

When Christmas Eve arrived, I set the crèche in its place of honor. The injured unicorn knelt at the manger.

With lion in pocket, I joined the processional. Passing the unicorn I whispered, "My imagination is tired tonight, little friend. Gift me with a story."

This is the unicorn's gift.

The Lion Who Feared

THE LION HAD SPENT MOST OF HIS LIFE developing his roar. He was not a happy beast.

His father had given him little attention as a cub—being intent upon strengthening his own position as the king of all the beasts in the immediate area through skilled lionic diplomacy.

His mother was a dreamer who spent hours watching imaginary landscapes in the clouds and wishing she were there.

His brothers and sisters teased him unmercifully because one front leg was a bit shorter than the other. He rolled in an odd way as he walked.

The lion became a loner. He spent hours hidden in a cave developing a ferocious roar. When he was ready, he stood at the top of a low hill. The sound of his angry voice reverberated off the nearby cliffs.

Shepherds gathered their flocks in anxious knots. Ravens dropped from flight in sheer fright.

The lion was pleased. He too could rule the countryside. He would not reign by his father's diplomacy but with the weapon of fear.

His tactic worked. Sheepherders put extra sharp-horned rams on guard duty with the flocks. As the lion's roar engulfed fields and villages, unwise parents would say to troubled children, "You do what I tell you, or I'll leave you out for the lion to eat!"

One cold winter's day, the troubled beast stood on a hilltop watching unusually large crowds streaming toward a nearby town. He kept a sharp eye out for straying pack animals. He saw none. His hunger deepened.

When night fell, he quietly crept toward a flock of sheep, trying to avoid the guardian rams whose sharp horns could slit open the belly of a lion. If he was lucky he might sneak up on a lost sheep.

At that moment, the night silence was embroidered with angelic songs heard more in the heart than the ear. When the sky blazed, the lion momentarily wished for his mother. She would have loved the display. The lion saw the shepherds embrace in fear and hope.

When he sensed the words concerning a babe born in Bethlehem, he saw the shepherds choose prize lambs from the flock and, leaving a ram in charge, rush toward the village.

The lion followed. Surely something edible would stray into his path.

Just outside the city limits he observed three camels coming down a nearby road. Their riders were richly dressed. The lion paused, gathered all his strength, and let out the loudest, most ferocious roar of his entire life.

The camels bolted. One rider dropped a small, ornately carved chest, which bounced down a steep slope in the darkness. After a great distance, the riders controlled their mounts and turned them again toward Bethlehem.

The roar caused quaking in village inhabitants and guests alike. The couple in the stable clutched their child tightly and the kneeling shepherds hugged their lambs.

The lion limped fiercely down the main thoroughfare. Shouts of "The lion is coming! The lion is coming!" echoed through the town. Rocks and spears were readied.

The beast followed the scent of shepherds and lambs toward the stable behind the inn.

As he continued to slink down the cobblestone path, he found his way blocked by a unicorn with a golden horn. The lion paused. If he could avoid the horn, a fine feast surely awaited him. He paused for a moment to consider what a mythological beast might do to his digestive system, but he was hungry enough to eat anything.

The unicorn sang a soothing song:

> Come now in peace,
> O mighty beast,
>   I care for you;
> Come now in peace.

Instead of listening, the lion gave another mighty roar and leaped at the unicorn. The unicorn dodged to one side—but not far enough. The lion's claw caught him on the flank and flipped him end over end, his horn jamming itself into a crack between the stones. It snapped off at the base and rolled to the edge of the path.

Landing, the lion turned in a single movement, preparing to spring again. He saw the bleeding unicorn huddled on the ground. It still sang in a quiet voice:

> Come now in peace,
>   O mighty beast,
>   I care for you;
> Come now in peace.

Perhaps it was weakness from hunger. Perhaps it was lifelong aloneness. Perhaps it was the interweaving of the angels' song and the unicorn's. But the lion cried until his hard heart broke. Beating within it he discovered the heart of love that lies deep within all living creatures.

The unicorn struggled to his side and said, "Great beast, come with me."

The limping lion allowed himself to be led through the stable door. Light from the great star washed the marks of the lion's claw from the unicorn's flank.

The song swelled with the addition of the voices of the man and the woman by the manger and the counterpoint of the cooing child.

> Come now in peace,
>   O mighty beast;
>   We care for you.
> Come now in peace.

The lion and the unicorn knelt at the manger.

The heavy clop of camel hooves sounded on the stable path. The great lumbering animals appeared, with their richly cloaked riders.

The man in the lead commented mournfully to his companions, "You have your frankincense and myrrh to offer to the young king in the manger crib. I lost my gift of gold to the lion's roar. I come sad-hearted and empty-handed."

Then he spied something at the edge of the cobblestone path glowing in the starlight. Dismounting, he picked it up, and shouted, "I have a gift for the long-sought little sovereign."

His compatriots climbed down from their saddles. Together they entered the stable and knelt in the empty places, which seemed to be awaiting their arrival to the holy scene. The cow nodded her approval.

Cones of frankincense and a cask of myrrh nestled at the foot of the rude crib. In the manger straw itself, within reach of the child's questing fingers, lay the unicorn's horn, glowing golden in the starlight.

The Interlude of the Pig

THE DAYS OF DRAB NOVEMBER descended. We hungered for Advent light. Christmas music and theater pieces were in preparation.

The unicorn and I wondered if there would be an addition to the crèche this year. No sooner had we wondered together than Lucy appeared at the door.

She said, "Close your eyes and hold out your hand."

I did as requested, and felt a bit of fired clay touch my right palm. Eyes still closed, I explored it with my left index finger. I was baffled. Then my finger arrived at a tightly coiled tail. I knew! I opened my eyes to be greeted by a rotund little pig.

Lucy commented wryly, "I thought you might need a little extra theological reflection on this one." She disappeared.

I introduced the unicorn to the new crèche companion. He chuckled, "There's only one tale coiled in your heart where you haven't found it yet that will suffice for this Holy Night."

Here is the tale from that Christmas Eve—prompted, I'm sure, by the unicorn.

The Outcast Pig

THE ROMAN GARRISON NEAR BETHLEHEM bought provisions of meat from a nearby farm. It was run by a former general, a man of principle who had been demoted because of his refusal to order a search-and-destroy mission.

The man enjoyed raising pigs for the soldiers to eat. He took wry-humored delight in the disgust of his Jewish neighbors, for whom pigs were religiously unclean. Their faith forbade their eating pork.

One morning during slaughter time, a particular pig cowered in fear as she heard the cries of her dying friends. She quietly circled the holding field, anxiously seeking a way of escape.

The night before, dogs had dug their way beneath the fence and had attacked the pigyard before being driven off by the servants. In a clump of weeds, the pig discovered their fresh-scratched path.

She squiggled beneath the fence. No one saw her leave.

As all animals know, confusion is a fine cover for escape. She met up with hundreds of people heading toward a nearby village and lost herself in the crowd.

Entering Bethlehem, the pig turned down a cobblestone path behind an inn. She discovered a stable. "There should be fine hiding places within," she said to herself.

Stepping through the rough opening into the dim interior, she encountered a very bossy-sounding cow, who was pacing nervously back and forth and bellowing orders to the other animals: "Clean your hoofs! Brush your coat!"

She spotted the pig. An angry "Moo!" burst from her chest as she shouted, "Unclean! Unclean!"

The other animals shrank back against the stable walls. This was truly a disaster. In the midst of the impending chaos they would all have to say extra ritual prayers to cleanse themselves and their surroundings from the presence of the unclean interloper.

The cow attacked the small pig, horns thrusting, hooves flailing. The pig rushed to and fro, squealing in pain. Then she disappeared.

The cow paused in exhaustion, proud to have removed the offender.

Later that evening when the innkeeper showed the tired man and his pregnant wife into the stable, the cow, though resenting their presence, was glad the ritual cleansing had been completed. If a child was to be born in *her* stable, she wanted to remove all possible risks in the midst of this fragile world.

When the baby was born its mother held it in starlight for a long, long time. The father took his turn, embracing him warmly while the mother slept.

After many hours, the mother said, "Dear heart, we're both exhausted. Let the baby lie in the clean manger straw."

"I fear the cold is too penetrating," the father replied.

Looking at the kneeling figures encircling them, she said, "Perhaps lovelight and starlight will warm him."

She handed the sleeping infant to the man. She leaned forward to arrange the manger straw. It was warm to the touch. Surprised, she lifted a layer. Burrowed deep within was the pig.

The cow began to cry out in great consternation, "Uncl—"

She was stopped by a deep look from the woman, who said softly, "The whole world is being reinterpreted this night. When an outcast warms my infant's bed, the word 'unclean' disappears from language forever."

As she spoke, she stroked the pig's head in its favorite spot, right behind the ears. The pig relaxed and began to surface itself.

The woman laid the infant in the warm straw. It instinctively snuggled against its newfound friend.

Tranquillity descended once again on the Bethlehem stable.

The Interlude of the Ram

I HESITANTLY APPROACHED LUCY during Eastertide. "Is there a chance of another ceramic offering for Christmas Eve?"

"Yes. Do you have a suggestion?"

"I wouldn't want to get in the way of your creativity—and I like surprises. However, I would like to do something with a particular sound. You're a musician as well as a ceramist. You choose."

"I think I'll keep you in suspense until the last moment."

On the afternoon of Christmas Eve, I returned to my study to find the unicorn in deep conversation with an elegant ram whose horns curled magnificently.

I said to the unicorn, "I'm drawing a blank."

He responded, "Tonight, when the processional passes me kneeling at the manger, I'll give you some words that should provide you with the necessary inspiration."

Fortunately, I passed him between stanzas of "Adeste Fideles." In the momentary musical break he whispered, "Shofar: the musical instrument made from a ram's horn that was blown to call the Jewish people to worship."

When the appropriate moment came, this story sounded out in the candlelit church.

The Ram Who Remained

THE SOUND OF THE SHOFAR cut through the early-morning air, carrying the cries of the faithful to the gates of heaven itself. The crowds streaming into Bethlehem paused for moments of prayer. Then the long lines began to flow again.

As the shofar sounded its two-note call, the ram, following the yawning young shepherd, felt his elegant horns tingle. The shepherd paused, opened wide his arms to the morning sun, and prayed for the presence of Yahweh God as he minded the flocks.

The young shepherd knelt down, scratched the ram behind his ears, and said, "You should kneel when you hear that sound, my friend. It reminds us of the ram caught by the horns in the bush that saved the life of our ancestor, Isaac."

The ram liked this particular shepherd, who was always teasing him and touching him. Sometimes his humor was harsh. If the ram allowed a sheep to stray, the man would squat in front of him, grab him by both horns, and threaten, "If you let that happen again, I'll cut off your beautiful horns before you die and sell them to the first passing merchant. He will take them to Jerusalem and offer them to the Temple musicians in exchange for sacrificial doves."

The ram hoped the shepherd was not serious. He was fond of this man who owned two lead rams. The young shepherd had made an arrangement with the innkeeper in Bethlehem to keep one animal while the other was on duty in the hillside pasture. The shepherd left a companion in charge while he walked into town to effect the change of guard rams.

The ram enjoyed his rest time in the stable—even if it meant putting up with the idiosyncrasies of the controlling cow.

The day passed without incident, its beauty marred only by the clouds of dust which rose from the crowds still tramping toward the village.

At dusk the ram saw the outline of a lion. He stiffened in anticipation of an attack. The lion turned and loped toward the village with a curious, rolling limp.

When darkness fell, the young shepherd and his companions bunched the sheep together. The ram stood on a small hillock listening for danger.

What the ram heard was not danger but a sound that made his horns tingle anew. It was not the double-toned sound of the shofar, but a multi-noted song of crystalline voices coming from the clouds, which seemed to shape themselves into praising figures.

Turning his attention to the shepherds, the ram sensed they had heard the holy melody as well. They were clasped in one another's arms in a decidedly unshepherdly fashion, staring in awe at the sky.

The tip of a cloud shaped itself into a figure of breathtaking majesty. Words emerged from the song. The words told of the Christ born as a death-wrapped babe in a manger.

The song of praise resumed: "Glory to God in the highest, and on earth peace among those who please the Holy One."

As the glory faded and the clouds resumed their accustomed shapes, the young shepherd urged his companion to choose a lamb and head for Bethlehem.

The ram was delighted. Had his horns not tingled with the advent of the holy chorus? Surely he would be taken to worship at the inn stable manger.

As he began to follow the sheepkeepers, the young shepherd turned and said, "The flock cannot be left unguarded. You must remain, faithful friend. I'll bring you news of what we discover."

As they moved down the far-distant hillside, the ram saw a limping lion emerge and follow them toward the village. The distance was too great for a warning bleat to be effective.

The night was long and cold. The ram remained at his hillock listening post. He heard no song or marauding beast but only the cries of the night birds.

Then he saw it: a silent lion bounding over the rocky earth toward his flock. This lion had no injury-laden lope.

The lion slowed to a belly-dragging creep, heading for the lead ewe. He was so focused on his prey that he did not see the ram move from the hillock to a defensive position.

As the lion leapt at the ewe, the ram reared back and raked his razor-sharp horns across the attacker's soft underbelly. The lion, ripped open, landed short of its prey, directly in front of the ram. With its last strength it turned its great head and clamped its teeth on the throat of the startled ram.

The knifelike incisors cut the life-vein in the ram's throat. The beasts sank to the ground, locked together in their final dying moments.

The ram glanced at the sky as consciousness ebbed away. He felt his horns tingle, saw the clouds reshape themselves into winged hope-bearers, and heard again the angelic song of peace to those who remained faithful in their tasks.

The next morning the young shepherd and his companion discovered their flock fearfully huddled in a nearby cave. The shepherd looked up the hillside and saw two motionless forms lying together.

Running up the slope, he discovered the lion and the ram lying in a pool of mingled blood. He touched the horn of the ram and said in the midst of his tears, "Well done, faithful one. You laid down your life for your friends."

The horn seemed to tingle at his touch. He chiseled the curled spikes from his prize ram and placed the finest one in his pouch, to be carved later into a two-noted instrument of holy praise. The other he hung on a nearby tree to remind him of his valiant friend.

Years passed. The shepherd, grown to manhood, was in Jerusalem for the Jewish festival of Passover. The crowds rivaled those he'd known that sacred night long ago.

He heard shouting and ribald laughter. Following the sound, he discovered a group of citizens and soldiers jeering at a cross-carrying figure. The shepherd recognized the man as the Storyteller he'd often heard. He couldn't understand why such a man who spoke only of love should be walking the criminal's trail toward Golgotha, the trash-surrounded place of execution. His hand fell to the carved ram's horn ever on his belt. The horn seemed to vibrate.

He followed the procession of doom. On a garbage-littered hilltop three crosses were raised. Early darkness descended. A cry of submission echoed from the cross in the center.

The shepherd fled.

On the first day of the following week he sought a place of refuge in a hillside garden pocked with tombs. It was still dark. Birds tentatively practiced their morning songs.

The eastern sky lightened. The shepherd raised the ram's-horn shofar to his lips. It tingled strangely.

He blew the ancient call which welcomed the sun. The strong blast dislodged a great stone, which rolled from the opening of one of the tombs. A man stepped out of the darkness within. He yawned, stretched, turned to the shepherd, and gave him a quick smile of thanks.

It was the Storyteller.

The Interlude of the Evergreen

MID-DECEMBER GAVE NEW MEANING to the lyrics "In the bleak mid-winter . . ."

Lucy had not delivered a new animal for the crèche. I did not want to press her.

As if cued by my unspoken concern, she entered our office quite unceremoniously and placed on our desk a ceramic evergreen.

I protested, "It's not an animal! It will be hopelessly out of place in the story sequence."

She responded, "Did I not hear you define creativity as the ability to place disparate elements in some kind of harmony. I'm just testing your creativity."

"Lucy, you can't do this to me."

"Rog, if you protest too much, some year I'm really going to get you. I'm going to hand you the object wrapped in Christmas paper as you go down the aisle to tell the story. When you open it you'll discover a second baby. That will be your real test."

"Oh no! I'll settle for the evergreen."

She left, smiling her enigmatic smile.

I stepped into the sanctuary. The twenty-five-foot tree with its cascades of white lights touched the ceiling.

I gave a word of instruction to the person in charge of lighting. I could hardly wait for the Holy Night.

The unicorn was delighted with my fine humor as I passed him kneeling at the manger on Christmas Eve. He winked and whispered conspiratorially, "I've been behind this all along, you know."

I winked back and shared this tale.

The Saving of the Evergreen

DURING THE DAYS AFTER THE BIRTH in the Bethlehem manger, a gentle rain fell. The pig loved it. The ground immediately in front of the stable door had been beaten soft by the feet of shepherds and sheep and camels and kings.

The rain turned the worn earth into a lovely wallow. The pig lolled lazily in the dark muck. Emerging from a luxurious mud bath, she entered the stable. The cow became positively apoplectic.

"You may have warmed the Holy Child, but that does not give you license to track mud into my residence. Get back out into the rain and clean yourself off before you enter!"

The pig complied.

A major problem had developed in the stable. The star continued to illumine the interior with its peculiar intensity. The cock began crowing at three A.M. instead of dawn. The cow gave down her milk at odd hours.

The baby simply could not sleep in the light. The mother shaded the child's eyes with a shawl till she tired. The father tried to find a place to cast a shadow across the fussy infant, but the angle of the starlight was all wrong.

One morning, as the sound of the shofar rang out calling all hearers to morning prayer, the father exploded, "Yahweh God, if you are really there heeding our cries, heed the cries of my son and the exhaustion of his parents. Send *something* to shade us from your great light!"

The sacred seed must have fallen from the hem of a king's robe. It found a home in the soft mud stirred by the pig. At the father's lamentation the seed began to grow. A staunch green sprout pushed beyond the surface of the wallow.

The pig watched in amazement as the sprout became a bush and then a tree. The tree grew taller and taller until it dwarfed the stable and shadowed the star.

The crying child quieted. The parents napped.

The cow was almost forced once again to confront the miraculous. Instead, she turned to the entering pig and absent-mindedly licked a dark fleck from behind its left ear.

Days passed. Dreams came to the father: dreams of terror and travels to distant lands. The couple left with the baby, conveying their deepest thanks to the innkeeper.

The innkeeper stood in his courtyard looking at the stable. The star had disappeared. The man stared at the tall tree. It looked as if it might one day push over the stable. The evergreen was no longer needed.

He picked up his ax and headed across the courtyard.

He was observed by a herald angel flying overhead. The heavenly being had enjoyed filling the shepherds with awe on the Holy Night. She was returning to the hillside sky to try again.

When she understood the innkeeper's intent she was horrified: he was going to cut down the tree that had shaded the infant Savior.

As the innkeeper readied himself to take the initial swing at the tree, the angel pointed a commanding finger. The tree was instantly illumined by a thousand lights.

The innkeeper fell to his knees, knowing he was doing obeisance in holy mud.

And that is why, even to this day, we dress the Christmas evergreen in lights.

The Interlude of the Turkey

"LUCY, I HESITATE TO MAKE A SUGGESTION, reluctant as I am to truncate your creativity. However, since I've already had doves cooing in stable rafters and ravens falling from the sky in fear, I think it would be lovely to add a bird this Christmas."

She pondered my request for a moment and then responded, "You asked for it. You shall have it."

As she left the office, a cryptic smiled sparkled on her cheeks.

I was delighted with her cooperative response.

Visions of eagles and egrets and herons and hummingbirds danced in my mind. This story would be one of soaring majesty that would lift the hearts of the listeners. I was excited by the prospect.

Weeks passed.

I arrived at my office in mid-December. There was a note on the door: "The bird is on your desk. Lucy."

I unlocked the door, my hand trembling. I stepped to my desk, where I was confronted by a small bird—the most indescribably ugly, scraggly, beady-eyed *turkey* I had ever seen.

My heart sank. I wanted to revel in beauty. Instead I was cursed by this laughingstock fowl.

I shared my plight with the unicorn, but this time he was no help at all. He simply smiled and hummed a chorus of "All God's Creatures Got a Place in the Choir."

My mood had not improved by Christmas Eve. I stuffed the ugly fowl in my pocket and stepped a bit belligerently up the aisle like a ram leading a flock.

As the children tumbled forward for the story, I stared hard at the turkey. The unicorn stared hard at me. This story began to take shape in the mists of my mind.

The Gobbling Clown

THERE HAS BEEN A SERIOUS ERROR made in the history of hymnody. "The Cradle Hymn," otherwise known as "Away in the Manger," was *not* created by Martin Luther. It was composed by the cow in the Bethlehem stable generations ago.

The cow thought of herself as quite a fine musician. Her rich alto m-o-o-o-o-o caught the attention of all listeners. After the child was born, she decided to create a choral masterpiece to honor the blessed occasion.

She had drilled the denizens of the stable to lift their voices for other events. A goat from a nearby field was quite a respectable soprano. The donkey's baritone would be a fine addition. The ox could handle the bass line. If the melody was kept in the alto, all would be well.

The cow entrusted the writing of suitable lyrics to no one other than herself:

> Away in a manger, no crib for a bed,
> The little Lord Jesus lay down his sweet head;

The cow sings so sweetly,
The baby awakes;
The child in the manger much crying did make.

(Dr. Luther was passing a stable in Germany after Midnight Mass. Every animal was kneeling, and they hummed a haunted tune. Luther listened deeply and then dashed home to transcribe what he'd heard. In the process, he transposed some words from the original.)

One day as the cow rehearsed her sacred choir, a shadow broke the steady streams of starlight. Shivering, she turned to the large eastern window. There, perched high out of danger, was a horrendously ugly turkey.

The decrepit bird looked longingly at the community of hymning beasts.

"Dear cow," she said, with a politeness belying her appearance, "might I join in performing that unspeakably lovely song?"

The cow was flattered and responded, "Perhaps. What part do you sing?"

"Oh, I am most versatile. I'm sure I could sing any part assigned."

The cow was momentarily impressed. "Why don't you join the goat, singing soprano?"

"Oh, heavenly," sighed the turkey. "That was just what I was hoping for."

The cow gave the order, "Take it from the top."

All the animals began really putting their voices into the endeavor when they became aware of a high-pitched, discordant "gobble-gobble-gobble" ringing out in the early-morning darkness.

The infant, who had been lustily crying, stopped and looked around for the source of the strange new sound.

The cow shouted at the turkey in exasperation, "Please, listen. The sounds of your gobbling have distorted our entire anthem. Remain silent, turkey!"

The song began again. The baby screamed.

When the song ended, the turkey appended a long obbligato of gobbles which moved over wide ranges of the musical scale. The child stopped crying.

As the gobbling continued, the child began to giggle. He giggled and giggled at the appearance of the newcomer and at her song.

The cow was infuriated. "Leave this stable at once and never come even close to us again. Leave!"

The mother at mangerside stopped the tyrant's tirade. She said, "Quiet, cow! There are times when the dearest gift of all is the gift of laughter. The turkey has brought us that gift. Sweet bird, bearer of joy, hop down to the edge of the manger so my son can see you better."

The turkey clumsily did what she was told. The cascades of laughter from the humans and the animals were a delight to the great bird.

The cow was chagrined. She was also, for a fleeting moment, terribly lonesome. But she soon stepped out of her defensive corner and joined the laughter.

The Interlude of the Tortoise

I watched the great turtle move laboriously across the green lawn under the summer sun. Another object appeared to be following the toiling animal.

I walked closer. I discovered the strap of a Boy Scout canteen wrapped around the turtle's right rear leg.

I approached the animal from the front, making what I hoped were reassuring sounds. It immediately drew its head and three legs into its shell. The strap prevented the withdrawal of the fourth.

I knelt down and carefully unknotted the leather thong. I expected the leg to disappear within the shell, but it relaxed in my hand. I'd never really touched a turtle before. Its skin was pleasant and pliable as my finger stroked the crease left by the strap.

A head slowly emerged, followed by the other three legs. I stroked the back of its neck with my other hand. The turtle stared at me with trusting eyes.

I reached into the nearby flower garden and picked a scarlet rose. I laid it on the grass in front of the creature. It nibbled a petal.

Arriving at my office I announced victoriously to the unicorn, "I have my tale for Christmas Eve."

The unicorn looked disappointed. "You didn't consult me."

"I wanted to surprise you."

"But I am all-knowing. I cannot be surprised."

"Well, can't you momentarily suspend that portion of your all-knowingness that deals with the Rog Robbennolt Christmas stories?"

The unicorn's body tensed. His eyes shut tightly. After a moment he relaxed, exclaiming, "It's done! I'm ready for a surprise." I slipped into the next office, where the unicorn couldn't hear me, and telephoned Lucy.

I queried, "Lucy, have you fired a beast for Christmas Eve?"

"Not yet."

"I want a turtle."

"You want a what?"

"A turtle."

There was a long silence. Then she giggled and replied, "Would a tortoise do as well? I think you want to deal with a land turtle."

"You're getting awfully scientific with someone who deals primarily with fantasy. All right. It can be a tortoise."

"You've got it!" Lucy was chuckling as she hung up the phone.

A few days later I secreted the tortoise into the box with the crèche without allowing the unicorn to see it.

I went to the church on Christmas Eve afternoon and set up the manger scene in its place of honor.

I stepped into the office to fetch the unicorn and paused to look out the window. A heavy fog had set in. It was indeed the bleak midwinter.

My spirit dampened. The tone of the evening would obviously be affected.

I heard the unicorn's voice from his corner of the desk. "Rog, I've spoken to you three times and you haven't responded. What's the matter with you? Are you depressed?"

"Yes. I'm tired. The gloom outside has seeped within me. The joy of the season is shadowed at the moment."

"That worries me," replied the unicorn. "What's that going to do to the evening's story? Having suspended my all-knowingness, I haven't a clue what you're going to do. Why don't you sit down here at the desk and do a run-through. For the first time in all our years together, I feel the need to check this one out."

I turned from the grim vista outside and sat down in my desk chair. Perching the unicorn in the palm of my hand, I began this tale.

The Tortoise Who Carried
the Covenant

THE TORTOISE SAVORED WITHDRAWING into the sanctuary of her shell and listening to the songs of the Sacred singing at the heart of creation. The tortoise was a deep listener.

As she toiled down a Palestinian hill in the gathering darkness, her senses were particularly alive. Impending music drew her on.

Her progress was painfully slow. While the roads filled with unusually large crowds of people flowing toward far-off Bethlehem, she took refuge in a cross-country route.

Her progress was impeded by a length of heavy grapevine that had become entangled on her right rear leg. Try as she might, there seemed to be no way to dislodge the burden.

However, the tortoise sensed a deep-running purpose singing within her. She moved stolidly onward, not really knowing where she was being led, yet facing that uncertainty without anxiety.

Suddenly, the song within her seemed to lift skyward and join the cloud-shaped song far in the distance, centered around the light of a great star.

The angelic lyrics urged her toward the village of Bethlehem, where a heavenly king in human flesh was born to common folk in a stable. She was assured in her soul that she would indeed see the carrier of great promise, the long-awaited Messiah.

The song recentered within the tortoise. She felt pulled toward the holy spot far, far in the distance. She kept her slow pace, dragging her burdened leg, pausing only to rest and nibble at the sparse vegetation.

Time had no meaning to the tortoise. The sacred goal was sufficient: to reach the village of Bethlehem.

Months later she arrived at the top of the hill overlooking the village. Below was a frightful scene. Smoke rose from burning houses. The screams of women and the cries of babies were carried upward on the westering wind. Soldiers on horseback rode roughshod through the settlement, brandishing weapons and slashing at random. Occasionally they dismounted, entered a house, and emerged with bloodied swords.

The tortoise waited until silence and darkness fell together. She made her slow way toward the stable behind the inn.

She crept in and discovered a knot of frightened animals in a far corner. Approaching the cow, who seemed to be in charge, she said quietly, "I've come to seek God's own child born in this place. Can you take me to him?"

The cow shook her head sadly. "No. The mother and the father and the baby left long ago. Herod's marauders did not know that. They've killed every child under the age of three hoping to destroy the infant king."

"I must find him. Where do I go?"

"No one knows."

"Then I shall simply wander and hope for the gift of insight that will draw me to him."

The tortoise began her slow departure from the stable.

The cow watched her drag the heavy vine wrapped around her leg. The slaughter of the innocent children had given the cow a sense of life's vulnerability. The presence of the child had taught her compassion.

She called out, "Pause for a moment, tortoise. There is a goat in the pasture with very sharp teeth. She could cut through the vine and speed you on your journey."

The tortoise smiled. "Speed is perhaps not quite the right word. But it would be a delight to go my slow way unburdened."

The goat was summoned, and in a moment the tortoise was freed.

She moved through the stricken village and into the open country, leaving the sounds of lamentation behind. She listened carefully to the song within the sanctuary of her shell. It assured her that she would one day see the Holy One shaped humanly.

Her quest became the center of her life. She aged, but her hope did not. Though her body eroded with the passing years, her spirit did not waver, for she carried within her a promise.

One day the tortoise passed through a second scene of terror. She crept through a narrow gorge in the mountains at her slow, deliberate pace.

Ahead, she saw the road nearly blocked by motionless human forms. As she came closer the way was slippery with blood. Shields and spears and bits of armor were scattered everywhere. Young Roman soldiers had been engaged by Zealots. The Jewish freedom fighters had killed the armed men and made away with their horses.

She stared into a handsome young face lying on the ground, and she wept. The song within her became a requiem.

"Another slaughter of the innocents," she thought.

As she left the gorge and the mountains she felt a weight being dragged behind her. When she tried to pull herself into her shell, her right rear leg was blocked. She looked back and discovered the thong of a full wineskin wrapped around it.

For the tortoise, burdens gifted the bearer with fresh strength and insight. She plodded on, following the promise within her of a holy vision.

She entered the village of Bethany. Darkness had fallen. She dragged herself along in the harsh moonlight, impeded by the heavy wineskin.

She paused to rest. In a nearby house she heard forced laughter, as if those participating were trying to avoid inevitable pain.

In the light of oil lamps she saw thirteen men. The one at the head of the table stood. The laughter stopped. The tortoise gasped. The song within her shell shaped itself to the nuances of his voice.

He spoke of betrayal and forgiveness and new life. One of the men rose abruptly and walked out into the night. He stumbled over the tortoise, his foot flipping her onto her back. He cursed, and disappeared into the shadows.

The man whose singing spirit echoed in the helpless tortoise spoke to the figure on his left: "Peter, the wine is gone. I have one last story to share with you. I need a final full chalice. Go and see what you might find."

He handed Peter the rough stone cup. As the man continued to speak of the necessity of simplicity and of the equality of humankind, Peter slipped quietly away.

He saw in the moonlight the helpless motion of the tortoise's legs. He knelt at her side, forgetting for a moment his mission.

"Poor tortoise," he said, "let me right you."

Then he spotted the thong knotted about her leg.

"I'll untie this first."

When the knot was removed, Peter righted the tortoise. She lay in motionless exhaustion.

Peter spotted the wineskin. "I wonder if there's any left in it."

He uncorked the skin and filled the chalice. He held the mouth of the wineskin over the tortoise's head and let fall a few drops. She awakened with a start, feeling refreshed.

Peter carried the cup within and handed it to the one who had been speaking. "Master, a goblet of story wine just for you!"

The Master took a flat round of bread, broke it, and began to sing.

The song within the tortoise and the song from the lips of the man became one:

> This is my body
>   Broken for you;
> As I have lived among you,
>   So must you do.

He passed the broken unleavened bread. They each held a morsel in silence.

He took the cup filled with wine from the tortoise's burden. Again he sang. Again she became one with the singer and the song:

> This is my life's-blood,
>   A covenant for you;
> As I have loved among you,
>   So must you do.

He passed the cup. The remaining eleven each dipped their bread in the wine. The silence was broken only by their sobs.

Outside, her quest completed, the tortoise slowly drew her head and legs into the sanctuary of her shell. The music at the heart of creation accompanied her on her final journey. She lay motionless in the moonlight.

An Interlude before the Second
Tale of the Tortoise

As I COMPLETED THE TALE the unicorn was weeping. He sobbed, "It's a beautiful, moving story. You've captured the heart of the gospel. But it won't work for tonight. The children will come tumbling up the aisle to surround the crèche, eager for the new story with lights from the great tree dancing in their eyes. They will not want to hear about dead babies, dead soldiers, and a dead tortoise! Lighten up, Rog."

I became a bit smug and very defensive. "You've said I captured the heart of the gospel and it was a moving story. I will not endure the Good News as eternally happy jollies. What's more, there is only one hour before the service. I can't prepare anything else, and I'm too depressed to improvise."

The unicorn stared at me from the palm of my hand. "Rog, stop it! Listen to the voices created within *you*. Take me into the sanctuary and place me by the manger. I'll spend the next hour in prayer. I suggest you do the same. Then we'll play it the way we've done so many times before. As you pass in the processional I'll feed you a cue."

I took the unicorn to the silence of the sanctuary. As I arranged the figures with the unicorn in his usual place of honor next to the manger, it seemed that all their faces carried expressions of concern. Even the cow appeared to be worried about my emotional state.

I returned to stare out the study window. Snow fell, softening both the landscape of the city and the landscape of my heart.

The congregation began to arrive. Robed, I joined the processional. Just before we stepped down the aisle, six-year-old Sara grabbed my leg and said loudly, "Merry Christmas, Rog. I can hardly wait for the story!"

Neither could I!

"Joy to the World" rang out from the great organ. The acolytes, choir, and pastors stepped briskly down the aisle.

As I passed the unicorn, I paused and placed my ear close to his mouth. I did not want to miss a sacred message in the midst of the general rejoicing.

The unicorn spoke four words: "Jerijah, the dancing beggar."

As the children came tumbling down the aisle, I let the unicorn's words settle into my subconscious to see what might be stirred.

Here is the tale that rose to the surface.

The Tortoise and the Dancing Beggar

JERIJAH, THE DANCING BEGGAR, stood at the Jericho city gates shaking his rattler–sistrum. The noisemaker was used to express both grief and celebration. Jerijah's life balanced between those two poles. Passersby would toss a coin into his clay bowl or lay a bunch of figs on the ground. Blind though he'd been since he was twelve years old, he sensed their presence and danced out his thanks.

The old tortoise loved to watch Jerijah dance. She lived on a hillside outside the city. She would creep into a corner of the wall. She loved to draw inside her shell and listen to the music which sings at the very heart of creation.

Often the thud of Jerijah's feet on the ground and the rhythm of the sistrum were in concert with the steady songs she heard within the sanctuary of her shell.

One day some children found the tortoise and decided to play a game of catch with her. One of them missed. She fell on her back in the soft earth near Jerijah's bowl.

She felt both helpless and excited. She'd never been so close to the dancing figure. She heard harsh laughter as people saw the overturned tortoise by the beggar's bowl. They began to toss coins onto her up-turned shell.

At the end of the day as Jerijah groped for his bowl, his sensitive fingers touched the overturned tortoise. He removed the coins, weeping as he discovered the act of cruelty he had been unable to see.

Jerijah tenderly turned her over and crooned a lullaby to her.

> We must touch, little tortoise,
> We must touch, we must care.
> When we care for each other,
> We serve God everywhere.

He touched the sistrum lightly as he sang. The beat of sistrum and song echoed with the music within the tortoise. She felt whole.

A decree had come down from the emperor, Caesar Augustus. All people must return to the place of their births to be officially registered. Jerijah needed to make the long trek to Bethlehem.

The tortoise was troubled. The songs in her shell began to tell of an infant king to be born in Bethlehem, the city of David. How she wanted to go!

The following day she crept through the gate and huddled down next to Jerijah's bowl. His groping fingers found her there.

He laughed and said, "Every traveler needs a friend. I'll put you in my pouch and carry you with me to Bethlehem. I've found a group of merchants who'll take me along if I'll entertain them."

The following day the caravan left. As they neared the village, the song of hope deepened within the tortoise.

They encamped at nightfall so that they might enter the village the following morning.

As they sat around the fire sharing food, shadows attacked. From the surrounding hillside caves the robber band descended. Many of the merchants fled. Those who didn't get away were beaten, robbed, and left for dead. The tortoise's blind friend received a well-aimed stone to the forehead and lay motionless on the ground. The robber cursed as he discovered nothing in Jerijah's pouch or pockets. He kicked the tortoise out of the way and followed his fellow thieves back into the hills.

Fortunately, the tortoise landed upright. She crept as quickly as she could back to her fallen friend. He was breathing.

She searched for help. All she saw was a well-rounded wineskin lying on the ground nearby. She wrapped the thong around her right rear leg and pulled the wineskin until it rested against his motionless hand.

She crept to his ear and sang:

> We must touch, dear Jerijah,
>   We must touch, we must care.
> When we care for each other,
>   We serve God everywhere.

The tortoise's song was supplemented by another melody. The sky blazed with light. The clouds shaped themselves into heavenly singers who sang of peace to humankind and of a holy child lying in a Bethlehem stable manger.

The song broke through Jerijah's pain. He moved his hand, felt the wineskin, pulled it slowly to his mouth, and took a long drink of the strengthening liquid.

Bracing one hand against the ground, he pushed himself into a sitting position. He felt the tortoise nestled comfortingly against his hand.

He listened deeply to the angels' song. He spoke to the tortoise. "I'm in great pain, but I think I could make it to the stable if you would be my eyes."

They struggled toward Bethlehem, following the great star.

The eastern sky was paling as they arrived at the stable behind the inn. The cow had collapsed into sleep from sheer exhaustion. The kings, wrapped in their travel cloaks, dreamed of a secret journey they would have to take. One of them was snoring loudly.

It was the unicorn who first saw them enter. He spotted the tortoise nestled in the blind man's right hand.

The unicorn put the stump of his horn in Jerijah's left hand and led the strange pair to the manger. The blind beggar knelt.

The mother and father were startled awake by the newcomers. She reached for the tortoise exclaiming, "All of God's creatures visit our baby. What elegant patterns you have on your shell."

The father chuckled as he saw his son's fingers entangle themselves in the beard of the kneeling man. Then the baby grabbed for the bushy eyebrows.

Suddenly the tiny fingers moved across the surface of the eyes themselves. The lenses cleared. The blind beggar saw the searching fingers and kissed them. The baby laughed as he felt Jerijah's beard tickle his tiny palm.

The sound of the shofar cut across the silence, welcoming the morning.

The now-sighted beggar reached out to the woman to receive back his friend. He rose.

With the tortoise in one hand and his sistrum in the other, Jerijah danced in joy.

An Afterword: Jerijah, the Dancing Beggar

I RETURNED TO THE STUDY, the unicorn nestled in my hand. I sat down for a moment to watch the snowfall in the streetlights. The window candle illumined the unicorn's face. Though his eyes were wet, he was smiling.

"I think *our* story tonight was beautiful."

"Well," I responded, "Sara grabbed my leg at the end of the service and wanted me to tell it again!"

The unicorn's face took on a serious look and he began, "Rog, I hope you learned something about creativity from this evening's experience. I—"

I cut him off by rising abruptly and placing him back on the desk. I responded, "Please dear friend, no sermons. It's Christmas Eve."

The Interlude of the Pup

IT WAS EARLY SEPTEMBER. Lucy called for a Christmas consultation.

"Rog, we've been doing Christmas Eve stories the same way for seven years. I think we need to add to the mystery. I'm no longer going to reveal the identity of the story-object in advance. I'll wrap my offering in Christmas paper. You and the mystic unicorn can improvise together."

Before I could respond she hung up the phone.

The following December the unicorn was justifiably nervous as I set him and his companions in front of the manger Christmas Eve afternoon. A package wrapped in green foil had magically appeared on the low table.

"Rog, are you sure you want to go through with this? Please let me reveal the identity of the package dweller."

I responded a bit sharply, "No! Part of the fun of this night will be watching me unwrap the package. I don't want to cheat."

"Well, just what is your frame of mind? You seem a bit edgy. I don't want another experience like the first tortoise tale."

I laughed, "Dear friend, I'll have prayer time before the service. I have many good people handling the last minute details. Please. Your worrying is beginning to affect me. Just meditate quietly."

The unicorn closed his eyes. I left to robe for the service.

Members of the congregation entered the sanctuary hushed by its beauty. The twenty-five-foot evergreen, alive with tiny white lights, almost brushed the ceiling. The shadows cast by candles underscored the mystery of the poinsettias.

Children slipped up the aisle to the chancel to check out the crèche and its attendant mystery package. They returned to their parents, whispering excitedly.

After carols and prayers, the children were invited to come forward for the story. They crowded around the table, eyes aglow. I placed each animal in front of the manger scene with a summary line.

I elevated the package for all to see, took a deep breath to invite the Spirit to envelop me, and opened the mystery box.

There, nestled in the tissue paper, was the saddest-faced ceramic puppy I had ever seen. She crouched defensively, wary-eyed.

I looked at her for a moment. A tear rolled down my cheek as I shared her silently with the children. An audible comment came from their midst: "A-w-w-w, poor little puppy."

I moved into this tale.

The Saga of the Sad-eyed Pup

THE INNKEEPER IN BETHLEHEM was a stern-faced man whose entire life had been devoted to the pursuit of business. Neatness and order were his chief virtues. He and the cow in his stable shared a common spirit.

When his little daughter, Leah, asked if she might have a few moments of snuggle time he exploded, "Hundreds of people are pouring into the village for the census and you ask for my attention at a moment like this? Leah, as the daughter of an innkeeper, you should know better!"

Leah's face clouded. She responded, "Jared's family sheep dog has puppies. He said I could have one. If *you're* too busy to snuggle, can I bring a puppy home?"

The innkeeper, somewhat ashamed of his outburst blustered, "I suppose so, but strictly on a trial basis—and only after you've carried extra water from the well. And let me tell you this: if there's any disruption because of the dog, it's gone!"

Leah carried the extra water in record time. She dashed down the lane to Jared's dwelling, shouting, "I can take a puppy. I can take a puppy!"

Jared's shepherd father put an arm around Leah as she made her choice. "Care for her well," he counseled, "and she will care for you."

Leah dashed back to the inn, her arms full of warm, exciting wiggles and an exploring tongue which immediately found her nose. She laughed so hard that she nearly dropped her new friend.

She was still laughing as she entered the crowded inn. She quickly discovered that her harried father was *not* laughing.

"Put that animal down and bring more water immediately!" he demanded.

Leah put the pup in what she hoped would be an out-of-the-way corner.

"Stay very quiet, p–l–e–a–s–e," she whispered. "Don't get into any trouble. I love you very much."

For a moment the puppy lay motionless. Then she spotted a nearby table leg. Her teeth began to ache with the desire for a good chew. She crept on her belly toward the inviting wood and began to gnaw contentedly. The wood was soft. Soon she had left imprints of her teeth all the way around the leg. She felt a real sense of accomplishment as a large piece of wood came off in her mouth.

A serving girl who had observed the puppy's arrival now also observed the puppy's activity. She moved quickly across the crowded room. Bending over she slapped the pup's head away from the table leg.

"If the innkeeper ever notices what you have done he'll wallop you from Dan to Beersheba. I'd better find Leah right away."

The pup cowered guiltily in the middle of the aisle.

But before she could head outside, the innkeeper called to the serving girl, "Four bowls of pottage for the customers in the corner."

She dashed to the kitchen and filled containers to their brims with the rich red lentil stew, remembering her master's caution that "Good measure keeps good business."

She hurried into the dining area and headed for the corner table.

She was so intent on her task that she did not see the crouching pup.

The girl tripped and fell flat. A tremendous crash accompanied her descent. The room exploded in rough, taunting laughter.

As she lifted her head from the floor, her face redder than the stew, her vision was crowded with images: a badly chewed table leg, shattered pottery, a veritable sea of pottage already beginning to turn the packed clay floor to slippery mud, and a puppy daintily nibbling bits of meat from the carnage.

The innkeeper roared across the room. Not stopping to assist his fallen servant, he grabbed the pup by the loose skin on the back of her neck. Stomping to the rear door of the inn, he tossed the quivering little beast down the path toward the stable.

As she flew through the air, the tiny puppy had only one thought: "I hope I don't land on the cobblestones."

Fortunately, she landed on a pile of straw for the camels which had been placed outside the stable by one of the magi. Shaking herself off, she crept inside.

It was chaos. A newborn infant whimpered. Richly robed kings were debating the significance of the moment in the harsh starlight. Shepherds were having a hard time finding anyone to listen to their wondrous story. The cow was trying to restore something like order.

Spotting the puppy, the cow cried out in exasperation, "I can't bear another living thing around this manger. Get yourself back into that corner. Stay there. Don't move. Be quiet!"

One cannot really say the cow kicked the pup into the dark corner. But she did encourage it rather harshly with a hind hoof. The pup cowered in its assigned place, absolutely motionless.

As the evening wore on everything and everyone settled into order under the cow's dominant direction.

Leah learned what had happened. She searched for her friend but could not find her. Too frightened by all the strangers in the stable to look there, she finally fell on her mat exhausted and cried herself to sleep.

Later that night, a kneeling shepherd, Jared's older brother, heard a discordant sound amid angel song and shining light: the high-pitched, frightened howl of a puppy.

His eyes searched out the distant corner. He recognized the puppy as one of the litter in his home. He was saddened by the fright which sharpened the little beast's bay.

He heard in his heart once again the angels' hillside chant. It had begun, "Fear not." On this night of nights, nothing in all creation need fear, not even a quivering puppy.

Jared's brother rose. The cow glared as the perfect scene was disrupted by his movement. Feeling that compassion comes before aesthetics, the shepherd moved to the dark corner, picked up the frightened animal, and sheltered it under his sheepskin cloak.

He whispered, "Because of tonight, nobody in the whole world need ever be afraid. That's what the angel said. I think it applies to you as well."

The puppy continued her quivering.

The shepherd went on, "Maybe it would help if you saw the wondrous baby."

Joseph was holding his infant son in his arms. The young shepherd reached the baby pup toward the human baby. The puppy's tongue found the baby's button nose. It smiled in its sleep.

At the touch, the puppy knew it no longer needed to be afraid. For one long moment she felt connected to all living things.

As the puppy reached out once more to lick a tiny hand, Joseph chuckled.

Even the eyes of the stern-faced Magi twinkled.

The next morning Leah found her puppy perched quietly in the lap of the dozing shepherd.

The Interlude of the Owl

THE DESK I SHARE with my co-pastor wife, Pat, is project-oriented. The stack to the left is most likely stewardship, or perhaps outlines for a church school staff meeting. A wedding ceremony balances precariously on the right. The center is most often occupied by sermon preparation for the current Sunday.

The unicorn objected to this slightly chaotic environment and often chided me about it. I would hide behind lame excuses about creative people needing freedom from ordinary strictures like order. He would shake his russet mane in disgust and make some comment like, "You're suffering from gargantuan carelessness."

Conditions always worsened at Christmas. Youth group scripts vied for a place with choir selections and lists for poinsettia delivery to persons who are homebound.

I rushed to the office before the five o'clock service more harried than usual. A young shepherd had lost his crook. I found him weeping in a dark corner of the hallway, grabbed a stuffed lamb from the nursery, and thrust it into his arms. He dried his tears on it and headed for the off-stage manger scene gathering. He was smiling broadly. I was not.

I quickly donned my robe and headed to the desk to grab the unicorn. He was nowhere in sight. I panicked, frantically shifting a few papers. Then I heard a muffled voice, "Try the third stack on the right."

I lifted a stack of scores for Handel's *Messiah*. There was the unicorn rolled on his side from the weight of the music. I picked him up.

He muttered on his way to my robe pocket, "That used to be my favorite oratorio until I was for all intents and purposes sacrificed beneath it. I felt absolutely caged."

I stopped his journey to my pocket. I looked him in the eye and asked, "Was I just fed a cue line for tonight's story?"

He grinned and nodded. We headed for the sanctuary.

As the children finished their enactment of the Nativity, they knelt around the ceramic crèche ready for this year's tale. I unwrapped the tiny package which Lucy had secreted on the table. It contained a curiously notched little owl. This story flowed out.

The Owl Who Found Freedom

Melchior's camel led the way because he bore not only a king but a compass. Suspended from a delicate chain between the two front posts of his camel seat was a gilded cage. From it stared a tiny, great-eyed owl.

When the three kingly wise men had met on the way from their far countries, the star had not yet appeared to guide them. Melchior shared a tradition from his people: "When one sets out on a sacred journey there is only one sure guide: an owl.

"An owl must be captured. Each morning special prayers are recited. The owl is then consulted. Whichever way it looks is the direction which should be taken. At the end of the journey the owl is sacrificed—killed in a special way—as a gift to the spirits who guided the owl."

As Melchior finished his story, his companions turned and looked out across the oasis flooded with the light of a full moon. The lead camel lifted his head from the water. They watched in amazement as a tiny owl alighted on the camel's head.

Melchior crept up to the feathered creature. The little bird allowed itself to be taken into his hands. Gaspar rushed to the merchant caravan drawn up near them and purchased a small gilded cage. The owl was obviously spirit-sent to be both guide and sacrifice.

Each morning the men consulted the owl prayerfully. Each morning the owl stared in the direction of the next leg of the journey. For days they had been heading due south.

One night, the light of a great star burst forth in the far western sky. The next morning the owl stared to the west. From that point on they followed both the owl and the star.

They arrived in the crowded city of Bethlehem. The owl quivered with anticipation and stared toward the stable.

Within they found the goal of their quest: a mother and a father—and cooing in the soft straw of the manger, a baby boy. The men knelt with their gifts. Melchior held out the gilded cage with the tiny owl. The baby smiled as the starlight made the owl's great eye's blaze with a secret fire.

Melchior reached within his robe and removed a slender knife. He chanted:

> We have been led to the center of life.
>   A sacrifice of thanksgiving is in order.
> We offer now the one who has in wisdom
>   guided us here.
> May the wisdom of the owl
>   become the wisdom of the boy.

Removing the bird from the cage, the old man lifted his knife. Joseph, the father, stepped forward quickly and grasped Melchior's wrist. He spoke sharply: "No! This is a place of life—not a place of death. Old ways are made new. Old sacrifices are unnecessary. Somehow the boy carries within him the wisdom of the ages. He has come to free those held captive—right down to tiny owls. He bears within him the true meaning of sacrifice."

Melchior relaxed his grip on the little bird. It spread its wings and, flying to the manger, nestled its soft breast feathers against the baby's cheek. The tiny one chortled in glee.

Then the owl rose on the beams of light from the great star. It perched on the edge of the opening through which the light streamed. It spread its wings. Its shadow embraced together shepherds and kings and beasts and the Christchild.

An Afterword: The Owl

I TOOK THE UNICORN out of the pocket of my pulpit robe commenting, "I think that was one of my best performances ever!"

I was about to place him atop Sunday's sermon. He scowled and said grumpily, "I've just provided you with one of our finest stories and I'm immediately relegated to the role of paperweight!"

I responded, "All right—where would you prefer to recline?"

"Put me in the windowsill under the electric candle."

"Why there?"

"Well, frankly, I look better in soft light."

He gasped and then, a bit abashed, said quietly, "That was an egotistic comment. I've been around humans too long. Like the owl, I'm supposed to lead folk to truth beyond themselves. Keep me in the window through the rest of the holy season. You could use a reminder on occasion of just what you're supposed to be about as a pastor. I'll help us both get beyond ourselves."

Chastised, I placed this ceramic extension of my conscience in the requested spot and turned off the overhead lights. We silently communed as the snow swirled against the windowpane behind him. Cleansed of our excursion into pride, I left him dozing and headed, homeward bound, into the windswept night.

The Interlude of the Swan

THE UNICORN HEARD MY FOOTSTEPS in the hall. He called out, "Rog, please don't turn on the light."

I s-l-o-w-l-y opened the study door. The little beast was basking in the incredibly bright glow of a full moon. His head was bowed forward so that the intensity of a moonbeam was focused on his damaged horn.

He said, "All this Christmas Eve day I've been feeling a shadow image of my missing horn. That misleading sense disappeared as the cool light flowed through the window. Now I feel enveloped in strange music. If you turn on the overheads, the song will stop."

I responded, "I just came back to get you. It's time for the service to begin. Perhaps this year you'd rather stay in your accustomed place on the desk—although that's a bit risky. One of the children is sure to miss you. Then I'd have to improvise "The Tale of the Missing Unicorn" as well as tell the tale of the animal wrapped in holly-printed paper that Lucy has left on the table with the crèche."

The unicorn bristled: "There is no way I'll allow you to tell a story without me present. You'd never get it quite right."

I laughed and took him gently in my hand. As I nestled him in the pocket of my robe, I heard a supercilious snort of self-approval.

We were met at the sanctuary door by Kyle, a rambunctious seven-year-old with eyes as wide as saucers. He shouted breathlessly above the joyous organ prelude, "Rog, something awful has happened. I just ran up to look at the crèche. The unicorn is missing. We can't have Christmas Eve without the unicorn."

Something between a happy neigh and a self-righteous purr erupted within the depths of my robe. Heads turned to observe the disturbance at the door. I whispered to Kyle, "I have the unicorn in my pocket. Don't worry."

Then a thought struck me. "Kyle, could you carry the unicorn very carefully and put him in his place within the manger scene?"

There was a gasp from my pocket and worried words tumbled out: "You're out of your mind! What if his hands aren't clean. What will happen to my tawny gold coat? Or what if he drops me? The remaining nub of my golden horn might be shattered forever."

I paid no attention to the outcry. I placed the little beast in the child's outstretched hand, which was quivering in sheer wonder at the chance of actually touching the unicorn. With the reverence usually reserved for processing the Host, the small boy, for the first time in his life, walked down the center aisle.

Seeing him coming, the organist segued into "Away in a Manger." The congregation held its breath as Kyle approached the three steps leading up to the chancel. He paused. As he placed a foot on each step the organist played a deep-throated ascending chime.

Kyle knelt before the manger scene and deposited the unicorn with that gentleness usually accorded a baby bird which has fallen from its nest.

The organ burst out with the opening hymn, "Joy to the World." As I processed by the unicorn, he looked a bit sulky as he quickly whispered, "When the service is over, please wipe the smear of licorice from behind my left ear. I've been so distraught I'll never be able to help you with the story. Well, it will serve you right for putting me in a threatening situation."

Later in the service, as the children tumbled down the aisle for their special story, I quickly dipped my finger in the baptismal font and sponged off the stain behind the unicorn's left ear.

I whispered, "Little friend, I know you've had a difficult day. You've already helped me with the story. It must be about singing light."

He smiled.

I unwrapped the holly paper. A swan glowed in the candlelight. I heard a song and told this story.

The Swan Who Carried a Shepherd

To HAVE BEEN BORN WITH ONLY A STUMP for a left leg would have been bad enough. But to grow only half as fast as one's fellows was the ultimate disgrace.

Jeresh's family had been shepherds since the time of ancestor Abraham. There was nothing else for the lamb-sized boy with a stick for a leg to do but follow his older siblings up into the hills with the sheep.

His grandfather had carved him a crutch out of a branch from a storied terebinth tree. Tale tellers from caravans would pause and ply their trade beneath that tree. The old man had carved tiny pictures of strange musical instruments on the little crutch. As he handed it to the boy he said, "Though your body may be lacking, keep this with you always. You'll hear heart songs."

Jeresh could circle a flock with the dexterity of a sheep dog while the other shepherds laughed at his clumsy grace. He would place the stick to his ear. Heart songs would drown out their laughter.

As the sheep grazed the Bethlehem hills, Jeresh heard music everywhere. He would place his stick against a granite outcropping and hear in his soul the song of creation's fire. The nearby oak sang a counterpoint of hopeful growth.

Jeresh loved the night watches. Granted, it was often a time of terror as beasts of prey sought to feed on the weak and the young at flock's edge. But it was also the time when he heard stories sung by the patterned stars. The other shepherds would listen to him humming along with the rhythms of heaven. Their laughter never quite erased the song.

One winter night light exploded in the sky. Voices sang. There was only one difference: all the shepherds saw the cascading brilliance and heard the voices. They huddled in the midst of the sheep while Jeresh scrambled to a high rock and greeted the appearance with joyous laughter. He lifted his crutch to the sky. The carved instruments played an accompaniment to the heavenly song.

The shepherds heard words about peace and goodwill sent from the Holy One, enfleshed and stabled in Bethlehem. They knew they would be particularly welcome in such a place. Jeresh descended quickly, saying, "Let me lead the way."

They shoved him roughly aside, remarking, "A cripple will only slow us down. Stay where you belong and protect the flock."

They rushed toward the distant village, having heard the words about "good will to all" without really understanding them.

A curtain of thick darkness descended. All the starlight seemed to flow toward a single point over David's distant city.

Jeresh crouched on the edge of an ancient stone whose top had been carved to catch dew and rain for the sheep. He wept. As his tears touched the water a silver sheen glowed across the surface.

Jeresh felt rather than saw a great bird descend and float in the tear light. A majestic swan paused at his side and said, "Jeresh, nestle yourself in the feathers on my back. We'll go together to Bethlehem."

He quickly did as the swan requested. The carvings on his stick glowed as they rose in the darkness. Their song joined the swan's song as they descended on the beams of a star over the stabled shelter.

The swan alighted fearlessly next to a great lion. Jeresh slid into the steely arms of his older brother, who immediately began to chide him for leaving the sheep unattended. Jeresh squiggled from the harsh grasp and half-hobbled, half-danced toward the wide-eyed infant staring at him from its mother's arms. The swan remained at Jeresh's side, steadying him with its strong beak.

He lifted his crutch in the intensity of starlight. Along with the great bird it sang a lullaby to the Child and to him:

> Fear not, my little ones,
> You'll not be shattered
>> By stable birth or cross death,
>> Crippled leg or hurting words.
> Listen for the heart song
> Sent from the Holy One.
>> Listen for the heart song—
>> Live hopefully forever.

Jeresh climbed on the swan's back. As they began to ascend, he looked down at his older brother. Tears moistened the rough-bearded face. Perhaps he too had heard the song.

The swan continued the lullaby as they flew toward the silver light on the distant hillside. Descending to the tear-dappled surface of the rock pond, the great bird floated there for a moment. Jeresh slid down the smooth feathers. The swan rose in the darkness, seeming to carry with it something of the surface's silver sheen.

Jeresh hobbled wearily to the flock. He nestled down next to an old ewe. Hearing the lullaby in his heart, Jeresh slept.

An Afterword: The Swan

AT THE END OF THE SERVICE, I recessed past the unicorn. He winked at me, obviously over his earlier momentary sulk. I reached down, picked him up, and nestled him once again in the depths of my robe pocket.

I was stopped at the door by Frieda McCann, leaning on her crutches. She looked at me wryly and commented, "I thought little crippled shepherd boys were always healed at the manger in Christmas stories."

I responded, "If I'd done that, a certain woman with crippled legs would have questioned my theology. I meant the story to be about listening to the sacred song inside and staying hopeful—which you've taught me to do."

She laughed in delight and hugged me.

I put my hand inside my robe pocket. My finger encountered a unicorn tear.

The Interlude of the Snail

THE UNICORN LOOKED PENSIVE. The late afternoon October sunlight transformed his tawny coat into sheer gold. I had been struggling with Jesus' words about the lilies of the field being beautifully clothed without the necessity of toil and forethought.

I closed the Bible and inquired of my little friend and mentor what he was thinking about. He responded, "I miss my sister. She was a problem sometimes. She was inordinately proud of her beautiful tan coat, which was as soft as silk. She spent hours staring at her reflection in quiet ponds. She flinched if a forest leaf fell on her back. She feared the presence of a stain.

"I used to tease her unmercifully. But now that I have been separated from her for a long time, I miss her. Now, don't take offense, Rog. You're very nice much of the time, but you're not a unicorn— particularly not my beautiful sister."

I was about to respond but, as usual, the telephone rang. I rushed to the hospital to deal with issues of life and death.

I could not get my conversation with the unicorn out of my mind. A few days later, hoping he had forgotten it, I said to him, "Little unicorn, do you trust me?"

He looked at me for a l-o-n-g moment. "Most of the time. But sometimes you get so angry that I fear you might sweep me across the room. After all, you are human. And surely in your travels you've seen the great tapestries that depict the hunting of the unicorn? It is difficult to trust humans. I love you—but trust is difficult."

He continued, "I'm sorry I couldn't give you a simple answer to your question. Why did you ask it?"

I chose my words carefully: "I wondered if you'd be willing to suspend your all-knowingness as it relates to our animal tales. I'd rather like to surprise you with a special story."

He looked at me quizzically and responded, "Perhaps I could do that a second time. Just promise me you won't get overtired and depressed on Christmas Eve."

I promised. I left him alone.

Stepping into a nearby office, I called Lucy. "Have you finished your figure for Christmas Eve?"

She laughed and responded, "Which Christmas Eve? I'm really into this. I've got animals ahead for many Christmas Eves. Why do you ask?"

I spelled out a special need. She assured me that she could honor my request.

When Christmas Eve afternoon arrived, I carried the crèche, the storied animals from previous years, and the little unicorn to the chancel and arranged them all in the place of honor. The cow jogged my flagging memory—as she always did—as to who went where. The unicorn insisted rightly that he should always be closest to the manger, since without him none of the tales would have emerged. The cow grudgingly acquiesced.

As I was about to leave the unicorn confessed, "I'm having a terrible time keeping my all-knowingness in abeyance. You know I hate surprises."

I smiled a bit smugly and left.

Just before the service I removed the new figure from its hiding place and nestled it in my robe pocket. When the children crowded around the manger for the story, the unicorn whispered, "I really do trust you."

That gave me just the confidence I needed to tell the story of the snail and the unicorn's sister.

The Snail Who Changed a Unicorn

S HE *KNEW* SHE WAS THE MOST BEAUTIFUL UNICORN in all creation—whether real or mythological. Her tawny coat was the silkiest, her hooves the most perfect shade of shiny ebony, her mane the longest to flow in the Mediterranean wind.

She spent hours staring at herself in crystal-clear tidepools. She avoided passing through olive groves, fearing that an overripe fruit might fall upon her flank and leave a permanent stain on the soft, velvety surface.

Now, you must understand: unicorns are creatures of great mystery. They never have a known name. However, this vain little beast had, in her heart of hearts, named herself "Aphrodite," after the most beautiful of all the goddesses.

Her younger brother was always teasing her about looking into the mirrorlike pools. She pretended to hate his attention.

One warm afternoon she stretched out in the sun to take her daily nap. She was careful to rotate sides from her sun nap of the previous day.

A passing giant snail spotted her shiny hooves and decided that one of them would be the perfect place from which to observe the boats on the distant sea and dream of far-off places. She slowly, laboriously climbed what to her seemed to be a small, dark mountain. She left behind, as snails always do, a narrow trail of cool moisture which the hot sun dried into a gray streak.

The snail settled comfortably onto her perfect perch. She watched the brightly colored sails in the distance. Since even snails can dream, she imagined herself in magic lands where the ground was perfectly even and snails could move with the speed of unicorns.

Suddenly, the unicorn awoke. She slowly raised her beautiful head and shook out her mane so that it flowed silkily in the soft wind. Then she spotted the snail dreaming on her hoof—along with the streaky trail it left behind.

She screamed angrily, "Get off my hoof, you filthy creature! You've completely ruined its perfect gloss."

She stumbled to her feet and flicked the offending hoof. The snail flew through the air. She bounced off a rock, cracking her giant shell, and fell to the earth stunned.

In a rage the unicorn galloped to the nearest tidepool, plunged in her stained hoof, and thrashed it about in the water, terrorizing the tiny sea creatures living in the pool.

Removing her hoof, she polished it carefully on a patch of thick lichen which grew nearby. Soon she could see her perfect nose reflected in its glassy surface.

Days later she risked another nap in a sheltered glen. She did not realize that the giant snail was painfully resting under a rock inches from her perfect ear. The snail had waited through long days for her shell to heal.

Suddenly, the unicorn was awakened by a tiny voice shouting in her ear, "Unicorn! Unicorn! Awake! Awake! The hunters are coming! The hunters are coming!"

She lifted her head and saw the snail. She was about to snarl at her when she heard in the distance the braying of hunting dogs and the savage music of searching horns. She saw a brightly caparisoned party, led by slender gray hounds, flowing into the far end of the glen.

She leaped to her hooves and galloped away as quickly as possible. A shower of arrows rained around her. One nicked her perfect golden horn.

A voice hissed from a nearby thicket, "In here! They'll never find us!" Her brother pulled her into a thick-leafed sanctuary. The haughty unicorn burst into tears of thanksgiving.

When the hunting party had passed, Aphrodite said to her brother, "I must find a certain snail who saved my life even though I harmed her terribly days ago."

Her brother asked no questions but simply followed her.

At sunset they discovered the giant snail. Aphrodite asked her forgiveness and offered thanks for saving her life. The graciousness of the snail overwhelmed the haughty unicorn.

At that moment a strange star blazed in the sky. All creatures within creation heard an exotic song—unicorns and snails alike. The song told of a holy babe to be born in the city of Bethlehem. All creation was called to come and worship.

Aphrodite's brother said breathlessly, "We must go at once!"

He was off, his hooves striking sparks on the granite cliffs along the seashore.

The snail said shyly, "I too would like to go and worship the Holy Babe, but it would take me years to get there. And besides, it's probably no place for a snail."

The proud unicorn paused for a moment and then said, "I'll carry you there on my back."

"Oh no!" said the snail. "It would take hours for me to climb on your back, and I would sully your fine silky coat."

The unicorn said simply, "I will wait. You must come."

She stretched out on the ground as close to the snail as possible. In all honesty she shuddered a bit as the snail's cold progress tracked its way up her side.

In a few hours, all was in readiness. The unicorn rose. Fire flared again from the rocks as they fled through the waning night toward Bethlehem.

As they arrived in the early-morning hours, the great star balanced the setting moon and the rising sun. Nearly all was quiet in the stable. The cow slept in an exhausted stupor, giving the newcomers a chance to choose their own places.

Joseph greeted them with a smile and a hushing finger to his lips while he motioned them to an empty place at his side.

He cradled Mary's head in his lap. She moaned softly saying, "Joseph, dear Joseph: the ache in my head keeps sleep at pain's length. Within the miracles of this night I need some ordinary comfort."

Joseph spotted the giant snail on the unicorn's back. He reached for it gently. The snail released the suction of its footpad which held it to the sleek surface. He placed the snail on the edge of Mary's forehead.

The snail rejoiced that it was created to move slowly. It made its cool way across the white field of soft skin. Mary sighed and said, "It must be an angel's soothing finger stroking away the pain."

For the first time that long night, Mary slept.

Joseph returned the snail to the back of the second kneeling unicorn.

An Afterword: The Snail

I NESTLED THE UNICORN, with the snail on its back, next to my friend. The two little beasts were both in tears. They nuzzled each other.

At the close of the service I passed by the crèche. My unicorn friend with the broken horn confessed quietly, "I'm glad I trusted you, Rog."

The Interlude of the Duck

THE UNICORN WAS STARING into the December darkness. He didn't even turn to greet me as I entered the office. A dismal drizzle had obliterated all hope of snow for the Holy Eve. Disappointed children were in touch with primal unruliness as I wended my way through the forest of askew halos precariously balanced on the foreheads of cherub choir members.

I quietly broke the unicorn's reverie: "Hey, little friend. It's almost time for our annual pilgrimage to the manger."

He responded gruffly, "I'm not going."

I was taken aback. "But this is the first time in ten years that you haven't prompted my storied spirit. What's the matter?"

"Lucy has absolutely departed from any tradition that makes an ounce of sense. It's an incomprehensible figure. There's no story that I can see."

Sirens raged in the street outside. Two police cars, an ambulance, and three firetrucks careened around the corner. The unicorn winced.

I counseled, "If you can't 'see' a story, perhaps you should close your eyes."

The unicorn turned toward me abruptly, a slight smile shadowing his face. "We've been together too long. You're beginning to think like a unicorn."

He closed his eyes. I put him in my pocket.

A half-hour later the cherub choir, having charmed the congregation, clustered around the crèche along with all the other children. Five-year-old Gayley Gribhorn had nearly upended me as she rushed forward and grabbed my leg. She looked up at me. I saw that her left eye was blackened and her cheek below slightly swollen. Her dad, Gus Gribhorn, had been briefly out of jail. They'd picked him up again earlier in the afternoon on a domestic violence charge.

I lifted her into my arms. She melted into my shoulder. Her halo fell off. As it descended to the floor it caught on my left ear and swung there for a moment. A wave of laughter broke over me from young and old alike. I could see I was in trouble. I looked to the unicorn for solace. His eyes remained tightly shut.

I picked up the holly-papered box containing four wrapped figures, and whispered into the child's ear, "Choose one, Gayley."

Her grin almost erased the destruction on her face. She chose the smallest of the packages and quickly unwrapped a tiny duck. She put it in the palm of my hand and melted back into my shoulder.

I looked at the unicorn. He'd opened one eye and was staring hard at me as if to draw my attention. When he was confident that I'd noticed him, he squinted both eyes tightly shut once more.

The Duck

THE TINY DUCKLING INSIDE THE EGG could hardly wait to break through the imprisoning shell and experience the world outside. What wondrous things she would see!

She felt life dancing within her. Kaleidoscopic pictures paraded in her dreams. Colors flowed and indistinguishable songs sang to the rhythm of her heartbeat.

She heard the cracking of shells around her and the excited exclamations of her released nest mates. The mother duck was teaching words like "sun" and "grass" and "water" and "waterbug."

Excited splashing indicated that a whole new world was being discovered. She pecked feverishly at her shell. She wanted to join the grand exploration.

Suddenly she felt the shell walls give way. She waited for the sights of the world to overwhelm her. She stumbled to the edge of the nest and toppled out, landing weakly on her back. She lay stunned. The reassuring beak of the mother duck righted her.

She turned her head from side to side, hoping to see. What she was experiencing now was no different from what she had experienced in the egg. At that moment she realized she was sightless. She sensed only what she had sensed from the beginnings of awareness: heartbeat songs which kept her from being totally alone.

During the months that came and went, she learned to fend for herself. She quickly found fine beds of floating duckweed. Her acute sense of hearing caught the slightest movement. She quacked a quick alarm when a fox or weasel crept near the birds feeding on the shore, saving them from certain death.

When the ducks moved with the seasons, her interior compass unfailingly took her where she needed to go. Sometimes she would blunder into a dry cattail stalk or tangle her webbed feet in a morning glory vine. The other ducks laughed derisively. Their scorn would be erased by a surge of that song within which assured her of her worth.

She had a special skill. Because she focused on voices and music and envisioned strange places upon the screen of her mind, she told wonderful tales.

She invented a history for pond dwellers. She told of songs sung within her by the Maker of all—songs which told how that Maker would weave self into creation. The other waterfowl were fascinated at the insights of their blind friend. They thought her stories both strange and strangely wonderful.

Then one day the duck fell silent. For three days she floated alone on the far reaches of the pond. The other fowl kept a respectful distance.

One night when the moon was full on the water the watchers saw her sail up a path of light. She seemed to disappear into the very moon itself.

They knew they would be lonely without her—but they would be sustained by the memory of her stories.

She felt herself directioned by shifting inner melodies. She flew into incredible warmth. The song sharpened. She heard heartening words about the Creator who wove peace into the mangered flesh of humankind.

She allowed herself to be drawn downward by the warmth. Her feet touched straw and she remembered the nest from which she had stepped into the world. She heard the sound of suckling lips and a mother's wordless song. The duck joined the song.

A woman's voice spoke: "Another comes to celebrate my son. What gift do you bring?"

The duck was silent for a moment. Then, prompted by the interior melody she responded, "I bring the gift of my blindness, which forces me to focus on rhythms and tales from the depths of creation which sing within all."

The woman responded, "My small blind friend, I am weary. Be my bard, my wandering teller of tales, bearer of ballads. Soothe both me and my suckling child."

A gentle rustle of sound poured from her beak as the duck sang of dancing light; of flowing streams and descending doves. She hymned an atonal tale of terror—of hammer blows and a rising cross and death's descent to a garden tomb. She pealed out hope of a stone rolled away and a Risen One.

Silence fell. The woman removed the sleeping child from her breast and laid him in the straw. She pondered in her heart all she had heard until dawnlight streaked the eastern sky.

An Afterword: The Duck

I LOOKED AT THE UNICORN. His eyes were closed. I sensed that he too was pondering. I slid Gayley to the floor and set the tiny duck in the manger. The congregation began singing "Angels We Have Heard on High."

At the conclusion of the service I returned to the chancel to retrieve the unicorn. He said sleepily, "Sometimes I just don't know how we do it!"

I snapped back, "We don't. God does."

He looked at me for a long moment and then commented wryly, "My, my! With insights such as that I expect to see a golden horn extending from your forehead any day now."

A quick trip to my robe pocket muffled further dialogue.

Then I noticed: something was missing. The tiny duck was *not* in the manger where I had left her.

As I knelt in bewilderment by the low table I felt a hand on my shoulder. It was Gayley.

She whispered, "I got somethin' for you, Rog."

She opened her fist. There in the palm of her hand lay the little waterfowl. She continued, "I didn't want her to get cold. I kept her in my hand 'til now."

The ceramic figured glowed with warmth from the child's palm. I promised, "I'll put her in my pocket with the unicorn. They'll keep each other warm."

She giggled. I gathered her into my arms. We graced each other with a healing hug on that Holy Eve.

The Interlude of the Goat

TED AND MARITA STEVENS had come to my study to discuss a Christmas Eve baptism. The baby cried loudly. The unicorn grimaced as he peered around a large Bible on my desk. Marita cast a worried look at the two-week-old infant son in her arms.

"I was so ill when he was born. I haven't been able to nurse him. We're still struggling to find the proper formula. He seems hungry all the time."

She laughed nervously. "My father said I should get myself a goat."

There was the sound of a sharp intake of breath from the direction of the desk.

I finished my conference with the Stevenses assuring them that I was not concerned about the crying of the baby. "The first Christmas Eve was not without tears—at least in my stories."

They laughed. At the sound of their joy the baby stopped crying.

When I was alone with the unicorn I asked him, "What kind of fuss were you making when I was speaking with the Stevenses?"

He looked at me innocently and said, "I wasn't making a fuss. I was merely clearing my throat. Is it against office etiquette for a unicorn to clear his throat?"

The telephone rang and I was spared further pursuit of the silly conversation. I forgot all about it until Christmas Eve, when the children gathered around me in the chancel with the crèche and its beasts before us. Eyes glistened in candlelight as I unwrapped this season's offering. It was a full-uddered milk goat.

I glanced at the unicorn. He was grinning broadly.

The Goat Who Gave

THE COW WOULD NOT—I repeat *would not*—allow the goat into her stable. She felt the goat was repellingly odiferous. But her terrible smell was not her only shortcoming, in the cow's eyes. She simply knew nothing about child-rearing.

The cow's calves and the goat's kids were studies in contrast. The calves were models of discipline, filling their days with strictly patterned activity under the iron-handed direction of their mother.

The kids, on the other hand, leapt about with unbridled joy, celebrating sunshine and reveling in rain while the goat looked on with rare aplomb, knowing that she would teach them to love and to care within the framework of exaltation.

The goat and her kids were banished to a shallow hillside cave, far across the field from the stable. It was often a bit lonely. However, they were assured of one bright spot each day: a visit from the innkeeper's daughter, who would arrive with her wide-mouthed stone jar to strip milk from the goat. She would play games with the kids and spend a bit of time scratching the goat's ears. The cow was jealous as she observed this activity from afar. But her general superiority made her certain that the innkeeper's daughter had very bad taste when it came to livestock.

When the city of Bethlehem filled with people and the inn filled with guests, the innkeeper's daughter served the goat's rich milk to those gathered around her tables. The cow was producing no milk at this moment of the year.

When the heavens filled with angelic voices and a great light, the goat rushed her kids to the top of a low hill so that they might remember the holy night as long as they lived. They saw, silhouetted against the starlight, arriving shepherds and questing kings. They felt for the time being that they were in the center of the universe.

Strange activity was centered on the stable. Leaving the kids to play King of the Mountain, the goat decided to violate the cow's edict of separation and creep close for a look.

As she approached she heard the wailing of an infant and the weeping of an exhausted mother. The woman choked out words between her sobs: "Oh Joseph, dear Joseph. I'm failing our son—God's son. I am so tired that there's no more milk in my breasts. He's hungry—so hungry."

Joseph took the Babe from its mother's arms, trying to comfort him and saying, "Rest a bit, Mary. Perhaps then milk will flow."

Some shepherds were just entering the stable. The goat quickly huddled in their midst, hoping the cow would not notice her.

She slipped closer to the manger. Joseph had carried the baby to an open rear door to shield Mary from its outcries. The goat noticed the large block from which soldiers in full armor mounted and dismounted their horses.

With a graceful leap she was on the block. If the man would only notice her distended udder, he might remember the value of goat's milk for babies when mother's milk is delayed.

She bleated softly to draw his attention. He looked first at her full udder and then at his sobbing son. He mused, "Perhaps it *would* work."

He folded his cloak on the block by the goat and laid the baby on it. The child's cries became more shrill.

Joseph gently reached for a goat tit and stripped out a bit of milk on his finger. The baby sucked greedily. Joseph milked a bit more into the palm of his hand and let the warm, saving liquid run down the eagerly suckled finger.

After two palmfuls of milk, the baby fell asleep on the folded cloak. Joseph nestled his infant son in his arms.

Across the stable the cow saw the goat standing still as a statue on the mounting block. She snorted, "Miserable show-off! I'll have her thrown out of my stableyard before she can say Caesar Augustus."

However, as the cow approached the block she saw Joseph put his arm around the goat's neck. The nanny goat gently nuzzled the infant's soft cheek. The cow heard Joseph say, "Goat, my dear goat: blessed are you among all creatures. You have nurtured our son—and should be ever praised. Stay here among us."

The goat replied quietly, "I have family to care for on the far hillside. I'll come again tomorrow to see if I'm needed."

She leaped from the block. As she turned, the light from the great star transformed her horns into burnished gold. She walked to the edge of its light. Then she disappeared into the night.

The cow was dumbfounded. The mere goat was to be blessed and praised? What a ridiculous idea! And then she saw the quiet Babe cradled in its father's arms and she knew something of a miracle had happened.

And the cow decided that on a strange night when the whole world was topsy-turvy, even the goat could make a miracle.

For the cow, that realization was her first step toward compassion.

An Afterword: The Goat

WHEN I RETRIEVED THE UNICORN after the service, he snuggled down into the palm of my hand and commented, "I hope I surprised you with the story. I doubt you remembered the moment with the Stevenses in your office."

"I had forgotten," I admitted. "I want all the stories I can find about the surprising places where compassion is alive. That's what the Holy Eve is really all about."

The unicorn's eyelids were beginning to droop. I slipped him into my pocket. Peace reigned once more—at least for the moment.

The Interlude before the Goose

IT WAS MIDNIGHT. As I drove up the street after three hours at the hospital, the great star that was mounted at the base of our church steeple beckoned me. I decided to pause and have a word with the unicorn. He would want to know about Felicity.

Felicity Andrews had just died in my arms. She was eighty-seven. The beat of her well-worn heart had simply faded into stillness. Alone most of her life, she had lived totally for others. She had worried that she might die on Christmas Eve, when "You'd be much too busy to bother with me, Rog. I'll try to time my exit more conveniently."

She'd been as good as her word. It was three days before Christmas.

Felicity loved the annual tales on the Holy Eve. One day while delivering fresh-baked muffins to me at my desk, she spotted the unicorn reclining next to the New Jerusalem translation of the Bible. She giggled and commented, "What a lovely contrast: the unicorn and the word of God. Now that's my kind of theology!"

She picked up the little animal and looked him in the eye, commenting, "A royal creature such as you should not have to lie down amidst the clutter of Rog's desk. I think I can remedy that."

Two weeks later she arrived with a gift for the unicorn. She'd grown up on a farm in northern Minnesota. Her father had taught her to hunt, and she was skilled at bringing down the great Canadian honkers that passed overhead each fall. Their down had filled elegant pillows. Her mother taught her to crochet elaborate designs with which to edge the pillowcases. ·

Felicity entered the study and laid a diminutive pillow atop the thick Bible. It was bright-red velvet edged with delicate ecru lace. Nestling the unicorn on the elegant object, she laughed and said, "A kingly bed for a kingly beast!"

I hoped she hadn't noticed the unicorn's self-satisfied smirk.

I thanked her warmly. In her usual self-deprecating fashion she replied, "It was nothing, really. I just opened one of my old pillows and removed a bit of down. The velvet was in an ancient trunk my grandmother brought from the east in a covered wagon. Fortunately my crippled fingers can still wrap around a crochet hook."

As I held her in my arms at the hospital, her final words had been, "Say goodbye to the unicorn. I'll see him shortly."

The harsh December wind tore at my face as I entered the darkened church. Approaching our study I heard staccato tapping. I peered through the half-open door. The streetlight outside the window shown dimly on our desk, reflecting off an oval of paper clips within which the unicorn was racing round and round as if he were performing in an ancient Coliseum.

He sensed my presence, stopped, and breathing heavily, commented, "Even mythological animals have to keep in shape." He gave a command and the paper clips flowed in a silver stream into their magnetic holder.

I spoke to him quietly. "Felicity died tonight. Her last word was a farewell to you. She said she'd see you soon."

His voice choked as he replied, "I already have. You caught me trying to outrun my grief."

On Christmas Eve the unicorn insisted that I take the goosedown pillow with us to the sanctuary so he could recline in splendor during the story.

When the children crowded around the crèche, I unwrapped Lucy's offering. It was a beautiful gray goose. The unicorn grinned and nestled deeper into the down. The story flowed freely.

The Goose Who Sacrificed

T HE GOAT AND THE GOOSE were the best of friends within the Bethlehem stableyard. Over the years they had nurtured kids and goslings to–gether. When the innkeeper had decided to serve roast goose to a visiting Roman general, the goat had helped the goose find a hiding place high in the rocky hills.

The innkeeper relented when the goose appeared with a fine brood of little ones.

The cow, as might be expected, did *not* approve of the goose's presence. Her personal habits annoyed the cow, and her friendship with the goat made her highly suspect. In her paranoia, the cow was certain the two of them were plotting to wrest her self-appointed throne from her.

Of course, the goat and the goose had never even discussed such a plan. All they wished to do was to live quietly and love whatever piece of the world they happened to be in.

It was most difficult to live quietly when great crowds poured into the little village for the census. The cow had heard a rumor that even the animals were to be counted. Everyone in the stable was frightened. The word was out that Romans would eat anything. The great animal count was merely a means to assist their menu planning.

When Mary and Joseph arrived at the stable, the goose observed them from a dark corner. She was now too old to produce eggs. Though the goat assured her that her real worth lay in her willingness to be a friend, the goose was practical: Everyone should be able to *do* something.

When the baby was born, the goose wept. She remembered her joy in each hatch of goslings. She felt even more worthless.

She watched the young mother wrap the baby in soft strips of cloth and lay him in the manger. She watched the baby squiggle, trying to find a comfortable spot in the harsh straw. The little one cried out in discomfort. Joseph quickly picked up the baby so the weary young mother would not be awakened. He stepped outside and awkwardly rocked his little one, unaccustomed as he was to this new task.

The goose knew what she could do. She was not too old for action. She sailed into the manger on her aging wings. Plucking beakful after beakful of down from all over her body, she had soon created a perfect nest of her incredibly soft feathers. Her body ached. There were touches of blood on some of the down.

Exhausted, she teetered on the manger's edge as Joseph returned. He welcomed the visitor with a smile. As he bent over to place his sleeping son in the straw, he was dumbfounded to see the gray-white oval. He nestled his infant in the soft down. The child slept soundly.

The ancient goose half-fell, half-flew to the ground and found her way back to her dark corner. She felt the cold penetrate her denuded body. Her old heart slowed to a standstill.

Grazing in a far corner of the pasture, the goat was suddenly aware of a burst of fire as the great star appeared. She thought she saw the outline of the old goose drawn toward heaven on a beam of golden light.

The Interlude before the Dove

I WALKED INTO MY STUDY Christmas Eve morning and was confronted by a very angry unicorn, standing on an open letter. He spat out, "I'm really feeling betrayed! I've suspended my all-knowingness at times when it comes to our stories. I've never interfered in your personal life. But this is too much!"

He pointed an accusing hoof at the epistle beneath him and continued, "I never read your mail. However, I needed to exercise so that my creativity is at its peak for tonight's story and the only open space in the midst of this mess was atop the letter. It was a little hard not to read it."

My heart sank. The letter outlined contract details with a retirement community where Pat and I were going to redirect our lives after thirty-nine years of active ministry.

Before I could open my mouth the unicorn continued his expostulation: "We've been together thirteen years. I thought we had shared deeply. Now you're going to quietly steal off somewhere and leave me behind. I'll be packed away with the Christmas things and forgotten. Your successor might well be offended by mythological beasts. I'll never see the light of day ag—"

He broke into piteous sobs.

I retrieved his red velvet pillow from beneath a hefty volume of contemporary poetry and placed him gently on it. I lifted him to the level of my face and spoke to him softly. "Little friend, I'm sorry if the letter frightened you. You know, sometimes it's hard to talk about life changes with those one loves most. I'll never leave you behind. In fact, I'm just completing a book of our stories. You're the hero of the volume. I want as many people as possible to know about you."

I reached for a tissue to dry his tears.

He took a deep breath and said haltingly, "I didn't really think you'd leave me. But even unicorns are sometimes afraid of change. Maybe that's what our final story together in this place should be about: understanding that we're never left alone no matter what changes happen."

I said cautiously, "Maybe you'd better reveal the contents of that final package wrapped in holly paper which Lucy delivered yesterday. We may need to talk this one over at some length."

"Let's go somewhere else to do it," he requested, giving the desk with its threatening letter a sidelong glance.

We stepped into the nearby book-lined conference room. We settled into the old oak rocking chair where I traditionally made the acquaintance of babies about to be baptized.

I perched the pillowed unicorn on my knee. He took a deep breath and closed his eyes in concentration. He then revealed, "It's a dove."

We rocked our way into the final tale.

The Dove Who Never Left

THE DOVE'S NEST HAD BEEN DISLODGED by a well–aimed stone from the hand of a soldier quartered in Bethlehem to keep order among the throngs of people inundating the village for the great tax count.

She had escaped injury. Her eggs had not. She hungered to nurture something alive since she would have no hatchlings to care for. The dove had long ago decided to open herself to both the seen and the unseen. She moved through life reflecting the sacred enfleshed in solid practicality.

She flew high over the village at nightfall hoping to avoid missiles from slingshots. Suddenly it seemed as if the sky was afire. A great star exploded over a simple stable behind an ordinary inn.

Amazed, she sought to become one with the light. She followed a star beam down through the ventilation hole in the stable roof. Exhausted, she alighted on a crossbar.

A strange tableau of sleepers stretched out below her: local beasts and shepherds, foreign camels and exotic kings surrounded an old man whose arm cradled a young woman clutching a newborn boy to her breast.

The only wakeful watcher was a unicorn. He turned the stub of his golden horn and shot a shaft of star-reflected light upward to the dove. Their thoughts communicated across the insubstantial beam.

The dove cooed inwardly, "I've flown into time's very center, it seems. There's more than meets the eye mangered below."

The unicorn responded, "Good woman dove, this peaceful moment is about to be shattered by a frightened ruler. Herod is plotting to kill the Holy Babe. Open yourself to the Word in the light. Hymn them some hope beyond fear."

The dove felt the light shape itself within her. She saw an outline of Egypt toward which the family trio below her made its painful way. Three camel-mounted Magi fled in secret directions. Interwoven with images of flight were the sounds of thundering hooves, weeping women, and fear-filled children.

The dove shared with the unicorn her light-borne vision. He responded, "Move quickly dreamward, dear dove. Move quickly dreamward!"

She moved within herself and cooed out an atonal song to the sleepers.

When they awoke, they were somber. Mary and the Magi discussed their common dreams. Joseph, always the planner, procured a donkey and provisions for their desperate excursion. The kings saddled up and disappeared in different directions to confuse mad King Herod.

Mary spoke to Joseph: "We've never ventured beyond the boundaries of our tiny land. How will we ever know the way?"

He responded, "Remember, Mary, the sacred words of birth and death were always prefaced by 'Fear not!' We'll know as we go. Something akin to a pillar of fire by day and a cloud by night will lead us."

As they left Bethlehem, it was Mary who noticed the dove circling high ahead of them, then swooping close, then moving far ahead in the direction they sensed they must go.

The dove never left them. She constantly companioned them in the far country. She dream-informed them when it was safe to return to their native town of Nazareth.

On a journey to Jerusalem when Jesus was twelve, the dove perched on the Temple high point and summoned his worried parents within. They were astounded to find him with great teachers probing those truths he would later live.

When the boy was on the brink of storied manhood, the dove sang him God songs as John dipped him beneath the Jordan's waters. Over and over she sang, "This is God's most pleasing, most beloved Son."

The song of the dove found its way into the hearts of many. Their lives became love-filled.

The dove never left the presence of the infant now grown to Storyteller. Her song sustained him, even when the crowds turned against him and he dragged a cross through the streets of Jerusalem.

She sang him a love song from the Father-Creator when the Holy Son cried out his sense of forsakenness on the cross.

Three days later in dawnlight she called him forth from the tomb and filled the graved garden and time itself with hope.

She perched on the rooftop of an inn at Emmaus and gave him the courage to reveal himself for all time.

Only a fisherman named Peter noticed, as the Risen One disappeared a final time, that only a dove remained. The hopeful song cooed into their hearts assured the onlookers that they would never be alone.

A few nights later watchful shepherds above Bethlehem saw the sky explode once more. To their amazement an ancient dove which had dozed for days in a nearby thicket seemed drawn toward heaven on a beam of light.

As she disappeared, they heard once again the words "Fear not" and "Peace is with you." They understood anew that they would never be alone.

An Afterword: The Dove

AFTER THE FAMILY SERVICE on Christmas Eve the unicorn and I slipped back to the old oak rocker. We sat in silence for a long time. Without speaking, we both knew we were listening to the last notes of the dove's song.

The unicorn spoke the final words. "Remember, Rog, wherever we go, together or apart, we need never really be alone."

I placed him on his red velvet pillow amidst a remarkably neatened desk. I left him glowing softly in candlelight.